ELIUD KIPCHOGE

A Journey of Discipline, Endurance, and Glory

Ronald C. Conlon

Copyright © 2025 by Ronald C. Conlon

All rights reserved. No part of this publication may be reproduced, distributed, or transmitted in any form or by any means, including photocopying, recording, or other electronic or mechanical methods, without the prior written permission of the publisher, except in the case of brief quotations embodied in critical reviews and certain other noncommercial uses permitted by copyright law.

Table Of Contents

Introduction
    The Greatest Marathoner of All Time
Chapter 1: Early Life in Kenya
    Childhood in Kapsisiywa
    Family Background
    First Steps into Running
Chapter 2: Discovering His Talent
    Meeting Coach Patrick Sang
    Training in the High Altitudes
    Early Competitions
Chapter 3: Rise to the World Stage
    2003 World Championship Gold
    Transition from Track to Marathon
Chapter 4: Marathon Glory
    Major Wins and Course Records
    Olympic Triumphs in 2016 and 2020
    Dominance in World Marathon Majors
Chapter 5: Breaking the Two-Hour Barrier
    The INEOS 1:59 Challenge
    Global Impact and Legacy
Chapter 6: Life Beyond Racing
    Personal Life and Family
    Philosophy and Discipline

Advocacy and Role Model Status
Chapter 7: Legacy and Impact
    Influence on Kenyan Athletics
    The Spirit of "No Human Is Limited"
Conclusion

Introduction

Many people consider Eliud Kipchoge among the best long-distance runners in history. Kipchoge was born in Kenya on November 5, 1984, and his remarkable marathon running accomplishments have pushed the boundaries of human endurance. In addition to winning major marathon competitions worldwide, he became well-known for being the first to complete a marathon in less than two hours, which he achieved under unusual circumstances during the 2019 INEOS 1:59 Challenge. Kipchoge is well-known for his self-control, modesty, and positive outlook. He personifies the spirit of excellence and tenacity, becoming a representation of what is possible with unwavering commitment and self-belief.

The Greatest Marathoner of All Time

Because of his record-breaking feats, steadfast discipline, and unwavering faith in human potential, Eliud Kipchoge is hailed as the greatest marathoner of all time. Kipchoge has set a benchmark that few can equal with his many big marathon victories, including gold medals from the Olympics, London, and Berlin. Even though it was unofficial, his unprecedented sub-two-hour marathon in 2019 captivated the globe and demonstrated that boundaries are meant to be pushed. Beyond his sporting achievements, Kipchoge has become a worldwide legend thanks to his humility, insight, and commitment, which motivate millions of people to strive for greatness with bravery and perseverance.

Chapter 1: Early Life in Kenya

On November 5, 1984, Eliud Kipchoge was born in Kapsisiywa, a small village in Nandi County, which is situated in the Rift Valley highlands of Kenya. This region is renowned for producing elite distance runners. Kipchoge was raised in impoverished circumstances by a single mother who was a teacher, frequently running several kilometers to and from school every day. He had exceptional stamina and self-control at an early age, qualities that would subsequently characterize his athletic career. Kipchoge started his quest for greatness on the dirt roads and hilly terrain of his rural homeland, where his love for running initially took root. He was inspired by Kenyan running heroes and received coaching from famous coach Patrick Sang.

Childhood in Kapsisiywa

Growing up in the sleepy village of Kapsisiywa, Eliud Kipchoge was characterized by hard work, simplicity, and an early affinity for running. Being raised in a low-income family, he was taught early on the importance of self-control and tenacity. Unbeknownst to him, Kipchoge laid the groundwork for his future as a world-class runner by running several kilometers every day to go to school, like many other kids in rural Kenya. He gained strength and endurance via daily living while surrounded by the Rift Valley's breathtaking scenery and high elevation. Kipchoge demonstrated focus and tenacity even as a young boy, qualities that would later establish him as a legend in the long-distance running community.

Family Background

Eliud Kipchoge grew up in Kapsisiywa, Kenya, in a modest and close-knit family. His mother, a teacher, was a major influence in his childhood and taught him the importance of hard work, discipline, and education. Kipchoge's mother raised him and his brothers after his father died when he was a small child, therefore he never knew him. His family remained very supportive and united despite the difficulties. Kipchoge's character was shaped by this supportive and resilient environment, which also laid the foundation for his future success on and off the track. His modest and grounded personality is still influenced by his family values and rural upbringing.

First Steps into Running

Eliud Kipchoge grew up in Kapsisiywa, Kenya, in a modest and close-knit family. His mother, a teacher, was a major influence in his childhood and taught him the importance of hard work, discipline, and education. Kipchoge's mother raised him and his brothers after his father died when he was a small child, therefore he never knew him. His family remained very supportive and united despite the difficulties. Kipchoge's character was shaped by this supportive and resilient environment, which also laid the foundation for his future success on and off the track. His modest and grounded personality is still influenced by his family values and rural upbringing.

Chapter 2: Discovering His Talent

Eliud Kipchoge grew up in Kapsisiywa, Kenya, in a modest and close-knit family. His mother, a teacher, was a major influence in his childhood and taught him the importance of hard work, discipline, and education. Kipchoge's mother raised him and his brothers after his father died when he was a small child, therefore he never knew him. His family remained very supportive and united despite the difficulties. Kipchoge's character was shaped by this supportive and resilient environment, which also laid the foundation for his future success on and off the track. His modest and grounded personality is still influenced by his family values and rural upbringing.

Meeting Coach Patrick Sang

Eliud Kipchoge's encounter with Patrick Sang, a former Kenyan Olympic medallist and one of the most renowned distance running instructors worldwide, was a turning point in his career. When Sang first met Kipchoge in 2003, he saw the young athlete's untapped potential right away and asked him to join his training group. Sang's guidance would turn out to be life-changing. Sang helped Kipchoge hone his abilities and comprehend the mentality needed to compete at the greatest levels of the sport by emphasizing discipline, organized training, and a balanced approach to both physical and mental preparation. Kipchoge's career took off as he started to climb to the top of the running world under Sang's knowledgeable tutelage. Kipchoge's success and longevity in the sport have been largely attributed to their relationship, which is based on mutual respect and trust.

Training in the High Altitudes

Eliud Kipchoge's training in the high-altitude areas of Kenya's Rift Valley was a major influence in his success as a marathon runner. The region's high elevation—more than 2,000 meters above sea level—makes it the ideal place to develop endurance and stamina. Running at these elevations makes the body adjust to reduced oxygen levels, which boosts the synthesis of red blood cells and enhances cardiovascular fitness in general. Like many other top Kenyan runners, Kipchoge trained mostly in these highlands, where he ran on rocky, mountainous terrain. In addition to improving his physical prowess, the difficult circumstances helped him develop a mental toughness that has been essential to his success in long-distance running. The foundation for Kipchoge's remarkable marathon career was laid by his high-altitude training, innate talent, and the knowledgeable coaching of his coach, Patrick Sang.

Early Competitions

Eliud Kipchoge's outstanding results in early events marked the beginning of his ascent to fame in the running world. He had his first significant breakthrough in 2002 when he won the Kenyan national junior cross-country championships at the age of just 18. His move from local races to more prominent competitions began with this triumph, which attracted the attention of the athletic community. Shortly after, Kipchoge raced in the 2003 World Championships in Paris, where he won a silver medal in the 5000 meters, giving him his first international exposure. His outstanding performance demonstrated his extraordinary talent and laid the groundwork for his future achievements.

Kipchoge had solidified his position as a rising star on the global scene by the time he was in his early twenties. He kept up his impressive performance in 5000-meter races, taking home medals and trophies from international competitions such as the World Athletics Final in 2003 and 2004. His decision to switch to marathon running, which would ultimately define his illustrious career, was made possible by these early events.

Chapter 3: Rise to the World Stage

Eliud Kipchoge's remarkable track and field accomplishments, especially in the 5000 meters, marked the beginning of his rise to prominence on the international scene. When he won the silver medal in the 5000 meters at the World Championships in Paris in 2003, it was his big break. Other triumphs followed, including a gold medal in the 5000 meters at the 2003 World Athletics Final, as a result of this early success. Kipchoge became known as one of the best middle-distance runners in the world thanks to his steady results in international events.

But it was his switch to marathon running that really made him famous throughout the world. When Kipchoge ran his first marathon in 2013, he placed second in the Rotterdam Marathon with a strong time of 2:05:30. He soon demonstrated his innate talent and strategic racing, winning his first marathon in 2014 at the Chicago Marathon with a personal best time of 2:04:11. With a string of triumphs, including the 2015 Berlin Marathon, where he established the course record of 2:04:00, Kipchoge's supremacy in the marathon persisted. He was a formidable presence on the international scene due to his unmatched consistency and capacity for high-pressure performances. Kipchoge had solidified his status as one of the greatest marathon runners in history by the time he took home the gold medal from the 2016 Rio Olympics.

2003 World Championship Gold

Eliud Kipchoge won the gold medal in the 5000 meters at the World Championships in Paris in 2003, marking a major turning point in his career. With this triumph, Kipchoge, who was only eighteen at the time, became a world-renowned distance runner. His performance demonstrated both his innate talent and his fierce competitive spirit.

Given his youth, Kipchoge's victory in the 5000 meters was especially noteworthy. He outperformed some of the top runners in the world, demonstrating his speed, tactical acumen, and mental toughness. This victory cleared the path for his future success in international events and cemented his status as a rising star in the sports world. It was a pivotal moment in his career since it showed that he had what it took to compete at the greatest level and hinted at the incredible accomplishments that would transpire later in the marathon and on the track.

Transition from Track to Marathon

Eliud Kipchoge's desire to test the boundaries of his endurance and take on more difficult tasks led him to naturally move from track to marathon running. Kipchoge was drawn to the marathon because it was a unique test of both mental and physical endurance, even though he was a formidable force in the 5000 meters, where he had already won numerous awards, including a gold medal at the 2003 World Championships.

After making his debut in the Rotterdam Marathon in 2013, he started running marathons seriously. Kipchoge finished second in a time of 2:05:30, indicating his promise as a marathon runner despite being relatively new to the race. His first marathon triumph came in 2014, just a year later, when he won the Chicago Marathon in 2:04:11. Kipchoge's career was defined by this triumph, which made him one of the world's best marathon runners.

Kipchoge made the switch to the marathon with ease, easily adjusting to the particular requirements of the larger event. He had a tactical advantage from his track racing background, and his unwavering attention and discipline carried over into the exhausting marathon distance. Kipchoge quickly rose to prominence in the sport by fusing the endurance needed for the marathon with the skills he had acquired on the track, solidifying his reputation as one of the best marathoners of all time.

Chapter 4: Marathon Glory

Eliud Kipchoge's path to marathon success has been quite remarkable. Kipchoge swiftly became the dominant force in long-distance running after a smooth transition from the track to the marathon. He made his debut on the international marathon scene in 2014 when he won the Chicago Marathon with a personal best time of 2:04:11.

As he earned victory after victory in some of the most famous marathons in the world, Kipchoge's genuine domination became apparent. He demonstrated his exceptional consistency by setting a course record in 2015 with a pace of 2:04:00 at the Berlin Marathon and winning again in 2017 with an even quicker time of 2:03:32. However, it was his triumph at the Rio Olympics in 2016 that made him a household name. Kipchoge solidified his status as the greatest marathon runner in the world by winning the gold medal.

Kipchoge's most famous accomplishment, though, was becoming the first person in history to complete a marathon in less than two hours in 2019. The INEOS 1:59 Challenge was a monument to his extraordinary endurance and mental toughness, forever altering the notion of what is humanly possible, even though it was not officially recognized as a world record because of the controlled atmosphere.

Discipline, humility, and an unwavering emphasis on progress have been hallmarks of Kipchoge's marathon strategy throughout his career. In addition to his physical skill, his marathon glory stems from his idea that "no human is limited," a philosophy that has motivated millions of people worldwide.

Major Wins and Course Records

A remarkable run of significant marathon wins and course records during his career solidified

Eliud Kipchoge's reputation as one of the best marathoners of all time. He has established a reputation for both genius and dependability in some of the world's most prominent races thanks to his ability to continuously compete at the top level.

London Marathon: There is no denying Kipchoge's supremacy in London. With each of his four victories (in 2015, 2016, 2018, and 2019), he cemented his status as the world's top marathon runner. His triumph in 2016 was especially noteworthy since he proved he could perform well on a fast course with a time of 2:03:05.

Berlin Marathon: Kipchoge holds a remarkable record at the Berlin Marathon. His victories in 2015, 2017, and 2018 created a new course record of 2:01:39, which at the time was the fastest marathon ever run. Because the flat, quick course fits his pace and tactics, his performances in Berlin have become legendary.

Chicago Marathon: With a timing of 2:04:11 in 2014, Kipchoge won his first significant marathon in Chicago. This victory paved the way for his subsequent triumphs and signalled his admission into the elite marathon ranks. Kipchoge's victory in Chicago is still regarded as one of his early career highlights, even though he has subsequently turned his attention to other marathons.

Olympic Marathon Gold (2016): Kipchoge made history by winning the Rio Olympics in 2016. He won the gold medal in the marathon with a time of 2:08:44, further solidifying his position as the top marathoner in the world, because of his exceptional endurance and tactical skill.

Course marks: Throughout his marathon career, Kipchoge has set several course marks, like as the 2018 Berlin Marathon record and his London Marathon triumphs, where his reliability has enabled him to dominate some of the most competitive fields in marathon history.

Kipchoge has been renowned for his tactical prowess and mental toughness in addition to his significant triumphs. He is a master of the marathon distance thanks to his ability to run races at the ideal pace and his concentration on steady, controlled effort. He is also one of the sport's greatest champions because of his exceptional consistency in major competitions.

Olympic Triumphs in 2016 and 2020

Eliud Kipchoge's Olympic victories, which demonstrated his extraordinary talent and unrelenting mental tenacity, have come to define his remarkable career. His reputation as one of the best marathoners in history was further solidified by his triumphs in the Olympic Games in 2016 and 2020.

2016 Rio Olympics: Kipchoge's triumph in the marathon at the Rio Olympics was a turning point in both his individual career and Kenyan athletics. Kipchoge gave a remarkable effort despite the difficult circumstances and fierce competition, winning the gold medal with a time of 2:08:44. His triumph was characterized by a blend of unmatched endurance, patience, and tactical skill. He performed an almost flawless race, keeping a constant pace for the entire 42.195 kilometers and gaining ground on his competitors in the closing miles. In addition to adding to his already impressive record of accomplishments, this victory cemented his status as one of the greatest distance runners of all time and made him an Olympic icon.

2020 Tokyo Olympics: Because of the worldwide pandemic in 2021, Kipchoge made a comeback to the Olympics for the 2020 Tokyo Games. The Tokyo marathon proved to be yet another difficult test, as the runners' stamina was put to the test in hot and muggy circumstances. But Kipchoge proved himself dominant once more. He became just the third man in history to win back-to-back Olympic marathon gold medals, defending his Olympic championship with a timing of 2:08:38. He overcame the race's environmental and physical obstacles to win his second Olympic gold, demonstrating his exceptional consistency, preparation, and mental toughness.

Not only did Kipchoge win the Olympics, but he also inspired millions of people with his self-control, humility, and conviction that "no human is limited." His status as a living legend in the marathon running discipline was further cemented by his two gold medals.

Dominance in World Marathon Majors

Eliud Kipchoge's unmatched consistency, tactical skill, and mental tenacity are demonstrated by his supremacy in the World Marathon Majors (WMM) series. Boston, London, Berlin, Chicago, New York City, and Tokyo are the six most renowned marathons in the world that are part of the World Marathon Majors. Kipchoge has made a name for himself as a dominant force in many of these races, frequently surpassing the top athletes in the world in some of the most competitive categories.

London Marathon: Kipchoge has had incredible success in the London Marathon. His four victories (in 2015, 2016, 2018, and 2019) demonstrated his command of the course and his capacity to run a race at the ideal pace. In particular, his victory in 2016—with a time of 2:03:05—was among the most remarkable of his career. His legacy in the World Marathon Majors series is mostly attributed to his triumph in London, which helped cement his status as a marathon champion.

Berlin Marathon: Known for its quick, level route, Kipchoge has been similarly dominant in the Berlin Marathon. In 2015, 2017, and 2018, he emerged victorious. He set a new track record of 2:01:39, the fastest marathon time ever recorded at the time, making his 2018 victory especially noteworthy. With Kipchoge showcasing his unparalleled stamina and speed on its famous course, Berlin has become one of his favorite locations.

Chicago Marathon: Although Kipchoge has frequently concentrated on the more well-known marathons, such as those in Berlin and London, he also won the 2014 Chicago Marathon, which was his first significant marathon triumph. Despite his sparse appearances in Chicago, this triumph was a significant turning point in his marathon career and solidified his position as one of the world's best runners.

Tokyo Marathon: Kipchoge's domination in the World Marathon Majors carried over to the Tokyo Marathon, where he excelled thanks to his remarkable endurance and controlled pace. His achievements in Tokyo have helped to establish him as a full-fledged marathon runner who can triumph on a variety of courses and continents.

In addition to winning numerous titles, Kipchoge's accomplishments in the World Marathon Majors have solidified his reputation as the most reliable marathoner of his time. For upcoming generations of marathon runners, his ability to win in a variety of situations and terrains while sustaining such a high level of performance has established a new standard. Kipchoge has established himself as a dominant force in one of the most demanding sports disciplines thanks to his cool-headed, collected manner and unparalleled discipline.

Chapter 5: Breaking the Two-Hour Barrier

Eliud Kipchoge broke the two-hour marathon time barrier, which was one of the most revolutionary feats in long-distance running history. At the INEOS 1:59 Challenge in Vienna, Austria, on October 12, 2019, Kipchoge accomplished what many said was unachievable by finishing a marathon in less than two hours. He became the first person to complete a marathon in less than two hours, finishing the 42.195 kilometers in 1:59:40.

This amazing accomplishment was a turning point in the sport, even though it was not formally acknowledged as a world record because of the controlled atmosphere (pacemakers and a flat, closed track). It demonstrated that the two-hour marathon was a real objective that could be accomplished with the correct mix of support, strategy, and physical preparation.

The result of years of careful preparation and training was Kipchoge's achievement. Advanced scientific support, such as hydration techniques, pacing equipment, and a group of top pacemakers who collaborated to keep a steady pace, were all part of his preparation for the INEOS 1:59 Challenge. Even though the event was designed to play to Kipchoge's strengths, it still took a tremendous amount of work to keep up the fast pace needed to surpass the two-hour mark.

The accomplishment demonstrated Kipchoge's remarkable athleticism as well as his fortitude and tenacity. It took a special blend of endurance, speed, and focus to run at that pace for more than two hours. Kipchoge's attitude was just as important to the challenge's accomplishment. He remained composed and steadfast in his conviction that "no human is limited"—a principle that continues to motivate millions of people worldwide—during the run.

The world's perception of the marathon distance was permanently altered by the

INEOS 1:59 Challenge, even though the time was not officially acknowledged as a world record. Kipchoge's accomplishment inspired competitors all over the world to set greater goals and test the boundaries of human ability by raising the standard for endurance sports.

The INEOS 1:59 Challenge

One of the most amazing occasions in long-distance running history, the INEOS 1:59 Challenge marked a turning point in Eliud Kipchoge's career. Kipchoge accomplished what was once thought to be an almost impossible feat on October 12, 2019, when he ran a marathon in less than two hours, completing the 42.195 kilometers in 1:59:40.

Instead of being a regular race, the challenge was a carefully planned event that was intended to provide Kipchoge with the ideal circumstances for breaking the two-hour mark. It was held on a level, closed-loop circuit at the Prater Park in Vienna, Austria. From the pacing plan to the scientific backing, every aspect was carefully thought out to guarantee Kipchoge could run the entire race at an average pace of 2:50 per kilometer (4:34 per mile).

The challenge was sponsored by the British multinational corporation INEOS, which assembled a group of supporters and professionals to assist Kipchoge in accomplishing this remarkable objective. To protect Kipchoge from wind resistance and keep a steady pace, a group of elite pacemakers alternated throughout the race in a well-planned arrangement. Additionally, Kipchoge had a "rabbit" car in front of him that provided real-time racing data and projected the exact speed.

In order to prepare for his best performance, Kipchoge had been working diligently for months, modifying his nutrition, training schedule, and recuperation techniques. In addition, the challenge included state-of-the-art equipment including hydration stations and pace cars, and Kipchoge ran with the help of professional athletes who were available to help.

The INEOS 1:59 Challenge was a historic occasion even though it wasn't a recognised marathon race. The two-hour barrier, a psychological milestone that many believed could never be crossed, was broken at 1:59:40. In addition to being hailed as a personal victory, Kipchoge's accomplishment served as evidence of human tenacity, self-control, and the strength of the conviction that "no human is limited."

Millions of people were motivated to push themselves and achieve their own lofty objectives by the event, which had an impact outside of the realm of athletics. The accomplishment enhanced Kipchoge's legacy and altered the perception of what was conceivable in distance running, even though the time was not formally acknowledged as a world record because of the controlled circumstances (such as the usage of pacemakers and a closed track).

Global Impact and Legacy

The influence of Eliud Kipchoge goes well beyond the realm of competitive marathon racing. His status as one of the most significant athletes of his generation has been cemented by his incredible accomplishments, especially his breaking of the two-hour barrier, which has had a significant impact on sports, culture, and inspiration worldwide.

Motivation for Sportsmen Around the World: Athletes from all disciplines have been motivated to push their boundaries and challenge expectations by Kipchoge's accomplishments, particularly his historic victory in the INEOS 1:59 Challenge. His motto, "No human is limited," has become a catchphrase for people who want to achieve greater success in both their personal and professional lives. Anyone looking to overcome challenges and accomplish remarkable goals may learn a lot from his unwavering focus, discipline, and commitment to self-improvement. Whether in running, business, or daily life, Kipchoge's narrative highlights the value of having faith in oneself and the strength of perseverance.

Enhancing Kenyan Athletics: Kipchoge has strengthened Kenya's standing as the center of excellence in long-distance running. Kenyan athletes, many of whom have dominated the marathon scene for decades, have gained even more international recognition as a result of his success. Kipchoge continues to coach younger runners as a role model, urging them to prioritize self-control, mental toughness, and tenacity. He inspires the upcoming generation to aim for comparable achievements by embodying the dreams of several athletes in Kenya and around Africa.

Cultural Icon: Kipchoge is a global ambassador for ethics and sportsmanship because of his character and humility, which go beyond his physical prowess. He has gained respect throughout the world for his humility and dedication to bettering himself rather than pursuing notoriety or personal honors. He constantly values hard labor over the chase of material gains and carries himself with dignity. The way Kipchoge has lived his life—with respect for others, an uncompromising dedication to his art, and a desire to have a lasting effect on the world—is what truly makes his legacy, not simply his accomplishments.

Impact on the Science of Running: Kipchoge's achievements have also influenced the development of marathon tactics, diet plans, and training regimens. He uses a combination of science, experience, and intuition when he runs. The INEOS 1:59 Challenge was a groundbreaking competition that demonstrated cutting-edge pacing, nutrition, and technological techniques. Numerous athletes and coaches have been motivated to push the boundaries of training by his rigorous preparation, which has deepened our grasp of the science of endurance.

Human Potential: Kipchoge's influence on how the world perceives human potential is arguably the most important part of his legacy. He stretched the limits of what was thought to be human endurance by breaking the two-hour marathon record. The idea of constraints in all facets of life is challenged by Kipchoge's ability to surpass what was previously believed to be impossible, and this accomplishment has spurred discussions about the boundaries of human performance.

Kipchoge is also dedicated to giving back to his community and beyond through philanthropy. He funds numerous projects centered on community development, sports, and education, especially in Kenya, through his foundation, the Eliud Kipchoge Foundation. To demonstrate that greatness is determined not just by sports achievement but also by the constructive contributions one makes to society, he works to improve the lives of young people and believes in the power of education.

In summary, Eliud Kipchoge's legacy and worldwide influence go beyond sports. In addition to redefining the boundaries of marathon running, he has personified the virtues of excellence, humility, and tenacity. Millions of people worldwide are still motivated by his accomplishments, and his legacy will endure for many decades as a brilliant illustration of the potential of people on and off the track.

Chapter 6: Life Beyond Racing

Eliud Kipchoge's life outside of racing is equally as motivational and significant as his marathon running career. Kipchoge has consistently kept a modest and grounded outlook on life despite his incredible accomplishments on the international front. His morals, dedication, and extracurricular pursuits reveal the depth of his personality and his ambition to leave a lasting impression on the world.

Family and Personal Life: Kipchoge's family is the most important aspect of his life outside of racing. He is a loving father to their kids and a devoted husband to his wife, Grace. Kipchoge has frequently discussed the value of family and how it provides him with security and emotional support. Even after his several victories, he can sustain his drive and focus because of the love and support he receives from his family. He frequently highlights how important his relationships and personal life are to his success and well-being.

Philanthropy & Giving Back: Another characteristic that sets Kipchoge apart is his dedication to giving back to his community. He supports several philanthropic endeavors in Kenya that center on rural development, youth empowerment, and education through the Eliud Kipchoge Foundation, which was founded in 2018. The organization seeks to promote a culture of excellence, discipline, and resilience while giving impoverished children access to school. Kipchoge's background in rural Kenya, where he learned the importance of perseverance, modesty, and community support, is the foundation of his desire to better the lives of others.

His foundation has collaborated with neighborhood groups to upgrade educational facilities, provide scholarships to deserving students, and advocate for sports as a means of fostering personal growth. Kipchoge has also underlined the value of education, arguing that it may help young people succeed in any sector they choose when paired with hard effort and dedication.

Business Interests: In addition to his charitable work, Kipchoge has dabbled in business, hoping to use his notoriety and achievements to create projects that will help his community and his long-term prospects. To further the ideals of excellence and discipline, he has collaborated with several businesses and groups, including those in the sportswear and sponsorship industries. His business endeavors frequently reflect his ideals, emphasizing sustainable processes and advancing topics that are important to him, such as encouraging fitness and healthy living.

Training and Coaching: Kipchoge keeps making investments in the future of marathon running even after he retired from professional racing. He continues to be actively involved in coaching young athletes, imparting his wisdom, experience, and insights to the aspiring runners. He guides numerous athletes through the difficulties of professional running and encourages them to adopt a focused, disciplined attitude to both training and life. The secret to Kipchoge's success has been his training method, which places equal emphasis on mental toughness and physical readiness.

Inspiration and Public Speaking: As a worldwide celebrity, Kipchoge regularly gives speeches in front of an audience to share his experiences and the lessons he has learned. His speeches frequently center on themes of tenacity, faith in oneself, and the quest for greatness. He has encouraged individuals to go beyond their boundaries by speaking at conferences on sports and human potential as well as corporate gatherings across the world. His message speaks to anybody who is trying to reach their goals, not only athletes.

Peace and Simplicity: Kipchoge lives a straightforward, tranquil existence in spite of his notoriety and prosperity. He continues to practice and lead the same strict lifestyle that enabled him to reach greatness, and he enjoys the peace and quiet of his rural house in Kaptagat. He has frequently stated that he appreciates calm and peace and finds strength in his community's support and the natural world. He emphasizes the value of keeping life in balance and is anchored by his simplicity and ties to his heritage.

Legacy of Hard Work and Humility: For Eliud Kipchoge, life beyond racing is ultimately about continuing to uplift, assist, and instruct others. His world records and marathon triumphs are part of his legacy, but what makes him unique is his humility, passion for helping others, and drive for personal development. He has demonstrated that greatness is not solely determined by accolades and records, but also by one's ability to positively impact others, uphold one's moral principles, and use success as a springboard to change the world.

Personal Life and Family

Eliud Kipchoge's personal life is distinguished by his close ties to his family, dedication to his principles, and profound humility. Kipchoge has always kept his personal life very private despite his enormous success as a world-class athlete, preferring to concentrate on the things that are most important to him: family, community, and personal development.

A Helpful Family: Kipchoge's wife, Grace, and their kids are the center of his existence. Kipchoge has frequently talked about how his family has been his pillar of support, giving him the motivation and the support he needs to succeed in his work. As a former runner herself, Grace has been a pillar of support for Kipchoge and is aware of the commitment and sacrifice required to be an elite athlete. Because of their collaboration, he can combine his personal life with his rigorous training schedule.

Kipchoge emphasises how his family gives him stability and inspiration, and he attributes a large portion of his success to their support. His children are also very important to him. Despite his intense commitment to his running career, Kipchoge makes time for his family, enjoying the small things in life and making enduring memories.

Humble Beginnings: Kipchoge's childhood in the Kenyan community of Kapsisiywa is a major part of his personal life. He was raised in a tiny, tight-knit village and was taught early on the importance of discipline, hard work, and family. Kipchoge's parents taught him the value of humility and respect, which he currently exemplifies in both his personal and professional life. He has never forgotten his roots despite his international recognition, frequently going back to his birthplace to support local issues and re-establish a connection with his community.

A Focus on Simplicity: Even outside of his running career, Kipchoge's lifestyle is characterized by discipline and simplicity. He trains and hangs out with his family at his humble house in Kaptagat, Kenya. Kipchoge leads a tranquil existence in the middle of nature, which gives him the calm and concentration he needs to continue exercising. This simplicity is a key component of his worldview since he thinks that living a simple life helps him focus on his objectives and stay grounded.

Work-Life Balance: Kipchoge recognizes the need for work-life balance despite his demanding training regimen and lengthy travel for competitions. He has discussed how realising that his relationships with his family and community are equally as vital as his athletic endeavours, he places a high priority on spending time with them. Despite the demands of professional sports, he can keep a sense of normalcy because of his family's constant support.

Family Values: Kipchoge's charitable endeavors are also heavily influenced by his family. He strives to better the lives of Kenyan youth through his Eliud Kipchoge Foundation, with an emphasis on sports and education. Kipchoge's foundation embodies his principles, and he frequently includes his family in these endeavors to teach them the significance of giving back to society. He has stated that he hopes to make a beneficial impact on future generations, particularly on his hometown, in addition to his sporting achievements.

The Kipchoge Legacy: In many respects, Eliud Kipchoge's personal life reflects the principles that have guided his professional life: diligence, self-control, modesty, and a strong bond with his family and community. His success is largely attributed to his family, whose encouragement has helped mold him into the person he is today. His deep sense of family and dedication to giving back is what characterizes him as a person, even though his athletic accomplishments have brought him international acclaim.

Philosophy and Discipline

Eliud Kipchoge's remarkable marathoning success stems not just from his physical prowess but also from his unrelenting dedication and personal attitude. His thinking has turned into one of his greatest strengths, and his approach to life, athletics, and competition has enabled him to do the seemingly impossible. In addition to defining his career, Kipchoge's philosophy—which was influenced by his experiences and upbringing—continues to motivate millions of people throughout the globe.

"No Human Is Limited" is a belief.

Kipchoge's well-known conviction that "No human is limited" lies at the core of his worldview. His training, race strategy, and overall way of living have all been motivated by this philosophy. According to Kipchoge, success comes from pushing past imagined boundaries, and the limits of human potential are frequently self-imposed. He has continuously shown that athletes—and, individuals from all walks of life—can achieve greater things than they first believed were possible provided they have the correct attitude, self-control, and commitment.

Kipchoge shares this idea with people in the sports industry and beyond, and it has grown to be an integral part of who he is. He thinks that if one is prepared to work hard, accept hardship, and keep a positive, unwavering attitude toward life, anyone can accomplish greatness.

The Strength of Self-Control

Perhaps the most crucial quality that has allowed Kipchoge to continuously achieve at the greatest level is discipline. His rigorous routines and unwavering dedication to his objectives form the foundation of his approach to training, race preparation, and everyday living. Kipchoge treats every area of his life with the same degree of discipline and focus because he thinks that success is based on tiny, gradual changes.

Kipchoge follows a rigorous training schedule that includes rest, mental conditioning, and food in addition to running. He follows a well-rounded schedule that emphasizes regularity and steady advancement. His ability to stick to a strict training regimen even after attaining great success is a testament to his discipline. He knows that excellence requires years of arduous work and constant effort, therefore he never takes short routes or demands quick fixes.

Focus and Mental Stability

Kipchoge's ideology stresses the value of mental toughness in addition to physical preparation. He frequently discusses the importance of mental toughness in long-distance running, particularly in the marathon. Kipchoge welcomes the mental challenge of persevering despite discomfort and exhaustion. One of the fundamental reasons for his success has been his capacity to maintain composure, focus, and calmness under extreme physical stress.

He exercises his intellect as hard as he does his body. Kipchoge stays focused and gets past any mental obstacles that can come up during a race by using visualisation techniques and positive self-talk. He has broken the two-hour barrier and accomplished other things that many thought were impossible because of his ability to tune out outside distractions, stay focused, and have a clear sense of purpose.

Gratitude and humility

Kipchoge is incredibly modest and grounded despite his record-breaking accomplishments. He thinks that success and ongoing development depend on humility. His goal in racing is to do his best and respect the sport he loves, not to gain attention or boost his ego. Kipchoge's contacts with his squad, other sportsmen, and supporters all demonstrate his humility. He never lets his accomplishments get to him and credits his family, coaches, and training partners for helping him succeed.

Kipchoge also cultivates thankfulness. He often says that he is grateful for the chance to race and for the knowledge he has gained. He is incredibly appreciative of his Kaptagat, Kenya, community and all those who have helped him along the way. Despite his widespread recognition and many honors, this attitude of thankfulness has kept him grounded.

A Simple Lifestyle

Kipchoge's ideology is evident in both his way of living and his athletic performance. He avoids the distractions of celebrity and financial prosperity in favor of a straightforward, orderly life. He finds tranquility in the outdoors and relishes the solitude of his Kaptagat home, where he trains. Kipchoge believes that leading a life that is meaningful and purposeful rather than one that is centered on appearances is important. His life is based on the principles of hard labor, discipline, and humility.

His running style reflects his simplicity as well. He concentrates on performing the fundamentals properly rather than pursuing lofty objectives or fame. Kipchoge is a strong proponent of consistency and repetition, saying that long-term success may be attained by doing the little things well every day. This simplicity and attention have helped him to retain optimum performance throughout his career.

A Tradition of Excellence

Kipchoge's concept aims to establish a benchmark for greatness that can be applied to all facets of life, not only winning marathons. His concentration on constant growth, mental toughness, dedication, and humility are models for anyone hoping to realize their potential. Kipchoge's message is unmistakable: a lifetime dedication to development, fortitude, and purpose defines success rather than a single accomplishment.

According to him, "The most important thing is to be humble and not to believe that you are a superhero." Greatness, according to his philosophy, is about staying humble and committed to the process of continuous improvement rather than being flawless. Kipchoge's example demonstrates that extraordinary things can be accomplished with commitment and discipline and that the boundaries of human potential are only as high as one is prepared to push them.

Advocacy and Role Model Status

As one of the greatest marathon runners of all time and a global spokesperson for tenacity, self-control, and constructive transformation, Eliud Kipchoge's impact extends beyond the realm of sports. Millions have been impressed by his life and deeds, and he has assumed a role as an inspiration to others outside of the athletics world. Through his activism, Kipchoge makes use of his position to advance environmental sustainability, social justice, and the principles that have guided his success.

Promoting Community Development and Education

Eliud Kipchoge is an ardent supporter of education, especially in his native Kenya. He thinks that the secret to enhancing youths' lives and releasing their potential is education. This belief is reflected in his efforts through the Eliud Kipchoge Foundation, which aims to nurture and educate impoverished children, particularly in rural areas. Kipchoge wants to make a lasting impact that goes beyond his sporting legacy by making investments in the next generation.

In addition, the foundation supports local community development projects, encourages youth to follow their ambitions, and makes high-quality education accessible. For many young Kenyans, Kipchoge's journey from modest beginnings to international prominence serves as a source of inspiration, demonstrating that they, too, can overcome obstacles and achieve greatness with perseverance and education.

Encouraging Environmental Awareness and Sustainability

Environmental sustainability has always been a priority for Kipchoge. He supports protecting nature because he understands the close relationship between environmental health and human well-being. His lifestyle demonstrates his dedication to environmental problems; he leads a modest and sustainable existence and frequently returns to his hometown, where he engages in eco-friendly measures like producing his food and cutting back on trash.

As an athlete, Kipchoge makes use of his position to promote sustainability in the sports industry. He wants to encourage players and fans to think about how their actions affect the environment, whether that is through his participation in clean-energy projects or encouraging eco-consciousness among his peers. The premise that environmental stewardship and human accountability go hand in hand is further supported by Kipchoge's example.

Set an Example of Self-Control and Perseverance

Kipchoge's support also includes his principles of self-control, modesty, and diligence. As a role model, he inspires people of all ages to embrace a persistent mindset and persistently work towards their objectives, regardless of the challenges they may encounter. His inspirational tale of perseverance begins when he was a small boy running barefoot in rural Kenya and ends when he breaks the two-hour marathon barrier. Kipchoge is a prime example of the value of remaining true to one's cause and overcoming hardship with poise and resolve.

Athletes and non-athletes alike can learn from his unyielding training discipline and racing philosophy. Kipchoge often discusses the significance of establishing long-term objectives, keeping the process in mind, and avoiding becoming sidetracked by short-term failures or setbacks. His narrative serves as a reminder that excellence requires consistent, daily effort in addition to talent.

Motivating Young Sportsmen and the Upcoming Generation

In addition to being an advocate for running, Kipchoge has a strong commitment to developing the next generation of athletes. He frequently engages with young runners in Kenya and elsewhere, providing them with advice and mentoring. He emphasises the value of maintaining discipline, believing in oneself despite obstacles, and having a clear vision. Kipchoge thinks that every young person may accomplish great things if they have the correct attitude and training.

Apart from his endeavors, Kipchoge has helped build Kenya's running infrastructure, which has made it possible for gifted runners to follow their aspirations. In order to create an atmosphere where future runners may thrive and represent Kenya internationally, he is advocating for increased access to resources, coaching, and training facilities.

Global Role Model and Global Influence

The influence of Eliud Kipchoge as a role model goes much beyond Kenya. People from all over the world find resonance in his story, which cuts across national and cultural borders. Kipchoge's message has motivated innumerable people to follow their passions and aim for greatness, regardless of their circumstances, whether it is because of his incredible accomplishments on the marathon track or his philosophy of excellence and humility.

As a world-renowned representative of running, Kipchoge has opened up the marathon to a wider audience, making it more approachable and motivating. Because of his incredible achievements, distance running has seen a resurgence in popularity, and competitors from all over the world are now trying to follow in his footsteps. Furthermore, anyone looking to shatter stereotypes and rethink what is possible might find inspiration in his presence in the global sports arena.

Leadership in Fair Play and Sportsmanship

Additionally, Kipchoge is a fervent supporter of fair play and sportsmanship. Kipchoge stands out for his commitment to competing with honesty and respect for the sport and his fellow athletes in a time when controversy occasionally overshadows sports. In both wins and losses, he constantly exemplifies the virtues of integrity, equity, and respect for others.

Kipchoge's actions set an example for athletes of all skill levels, whether it's applauding rivals after a race or being modest in the face of his many victories. As a champion and a genuine representative of athletics, he has gained recognition for his leadership in encouraging moral conduct in sports.

Legacy as an Example

Beyond just his sporting accomplishments, Eliud Kipchoge is a well-known advocate and role model. He is a representation of societal responsibility, discipline, tenacity, and humility. The next generation of leaders in sports and society at large are being shaped by his support of education, sustainability, and community development. Kipchoge's legacy will live on for generations to come, not just as the greatest runner of all time but also as a kind and significant global role model because of his dedication to inspiring others and using his platform for good.

Chapter 7: Legacy and Impact

Eliud Kipchoge left behind much more than just a string of world records and marathon triumphs. Millions of people worldwide have been inspired by his incredible career, which has permanently altered the long-distance running environment. As the all-time great marathon runner, Kipchoge's accomplishments go beyond sports; his influence touches on tenacity, self-control, and the conviction that human potential is limitless. His status as one of the most significant athletes of the modern age has been solidified by the impact of his achievements, both on and off the track.

Rewriting Human Performance Boundaries

Generations to come will be impacted by Kipchoge's influence on the marathon. What is deemed feasible in long-distance running has been redefined by his capacity to push the limits of human endurance and performance. In addition to breaking a significant record,

Kipchoge's achievement of being the first person in history to complete a marathon in less than two hours encouraged athletes of many sports to challenge their boundaries. In addition to being a feat of physical strength, Kipchoge's completion of the INEOS 1:59 Challenge marathon in 1:59:40 served as a testament to the strength of the mind, preparation, and faith.

This accomplishment altered people's beliefs of human potential and what athletes are capable of. "No human is limited," which Kipchoge's legacy has come to represent, is a constant reminder to strive for greater things and push past obstacles.

Changing the Marathon Environment

Kipchoge's supremacy in the marathon has also elevated the sport to a new level of prominence and awareness. Because of his unmatched speed and consistency, as well as his victories in the World Marathon Majors, the marathon has become a worldwide spectacle. As a result, more athletes are now aiming for greatness by running the marathon, particularly those from developing countries. Kipchoge's achievements have raised the bar for upcoming contests and encouraged the international expansion of long-distance running by motivating a new generation of runners to pursue similar careers.

Kipchoge has altered the way marathons are viewed both strategically and culturally with his methodical approach to racing, his record-breaking feats, and his unwavering dedication to training. His work has established a new standard for excellence that is probably going to last for many years.

An International Example

Even if Kipchoge's athletic accomplishments are revolutionary, his influence as a role model may be even more significant. He is an inspiration to individuals from all walks of life because of his personal philosophy of humility, discipline, and perseverance, which goes beyond the realm of athletics. Kipchoge's conviction that everything is attainable with perseverance, hard effort, and self-belief strikes a deep chord with others who are trying to overcome their obstacles.

Kipchoge has utilized his position as a global spokesperson for sustainability, education, and constructive change to promote issues bigger than himself. Young people have been empowered and given possibilities for a better future through his work with the Eliud Kipchoge Foundation, which focuses on educating and supporting underprivileged areas. Kipchoge has demonstrated that the real test of success is not just one's accomplishments but also one's capacity to raise and influence others.

Mental Capacity and the Human Spirit

The enduring mental fortitude of Kipchoge is among the most potent elements of his legacy. The marathon is a mental as well as a physical test, and Kipchoge has distinguished himself by persevering through the agony and uncertainty of a race. He is a ray of hope for anyone going through a difficult time because of his faith in the ability of the human spirit to triumph over hardship.

Kipchoge's path serves as an example of the strength of perseverance and mental toughness. His marathon triumphs have demonstrated not only how well-conditioned he is physically, but also how crucial a tough, concentrated mindset is to reaching greatness. His belief that the mind can occasionally overcome physical limitations has changed the game and inspired sportsmen in various sports to strengthen their mental toughness.

Impact on Culture and Society

Beyond the realm of sports, Kipchoge's influence may be seen in the larger social and cultural arena. As a proud Kenyan, his accomplishments have brought attention to Kenyan athletes, especially in long-distance running, and showcased the amazing athletic talent found in Africa. His triumphs have encouraged many young runners to pursue their goals and helped Kenya establish itself as the world's top marathon nation.

Kipchoge's modest upbringing in the town of Kapsisiywa serves as a potent reminder of the potential that comes with opportunity, hard effort, and persistence. He is now a national hero in Kenya and a source of pride for the African continent as a result of his ascent from lowly beginnings to international fame. His accomplishments have raised awareness of the social problems his society faces, such as poverty and education, and he has utilized his position to push for constructive change in his native nation.

Long-Term Impact on Upcoming Generations

For many years to come, Eliud Kipchoge's impact will continue to alter the running community and beyond. In addition to his athletic ability, future generations of marathon runners will surely look up to him for his moral character, self-control, and dedication to helping others. In addition to winning, Kipchoge's career has established the benchmark for what it means to be a champion in terms of one's demeanor, which includes humility, generosity, and respect.

Kipchoge's message of tenacity and self-belief has influenced individuals from various walks of life in addition to motivating athletics. Kipchoge's life story serves as a reminder to both business executives and regular people that everything is possible if you have the correct mindset. In addition to being a marathon runner who revolutionized the sport, he is remembered as a guy who altered people's perceptions of human potential and the spirit.

A Durable Legacy

Kipchoge has left an enduring impression on sports history and accomplished what many thought was impossible, making his legacy genuinely unique. His influence goes well beyond his marathon triumphs; it is a legacy of tenacity, commitment, and sacrifice. His impact will endure for many generations to come because of his extraordinary career and support of sustainability, education, and personal development. Eliud Kipchoge is more than just a marathon runner; he is a representation of what may happen when the human spirit is driven to achieve the impossible. For many years to come, his legacy will continue to inspire, encourage, and mentor countless people.

Influence on Kenyan Athletics

Eliud Kipchoge has had a significant, wide-ranging, and revolutionary impact on Kenyan sports. His influence extends beyond his achievements as one of Kenya's greatest athletes. His accomplishments have improved the nation's already stellar long-distance running reputation and influenced the direction of sports in Kenya and around the world. Through his accomplishments, work ethic, and dedication to the sport, Kipchoge has established Kenya as a long-distance running superpower, inspired a new generation of

Kenyan runners, and drawn attention to the nation's athletic programs internationally.

Increasing the Recognition of Long-Distance Running in Kenya

Although Kenya has long been known for producing great distance runners, Kipchoge's success on the international scene has increased awareness of the nation's long-distance competitors. His accomplishments have demonstrated to the world the breadth of Kenyan potential and the fact that Kenyan marathon runners set the standard. As the face of Kenyan athletics, Kipchoge has inspired pride in the country's great tradition of endurance running by setting world records and winning major competitions like the London Marathon and the Berlin Marathon.

Kenyan runners not only dominate, but do so with unparalleled consistency, as demonstrated by Kipchoge's numerous victories. With wins in more than 90% of the major marathons he has entered, his nearly flawless marathon career has increased awareness of Kenyan athletes, promoting greater international competition and elevating the stature of the nation's running programs.

Motivating a New Wave of Runners

Many young runners in Kenya and other countries now look up to Eliud Kipchoge. His ascent to international superstardom from the tiny village of Kapsisiywa shows that anyone can achieve the greatest success possible with talent and perseverance, regardless of background. His impact has demonstrated that hard work, perseverance, and discipline are the keys to success; there are no shortcuts to greatness.

Many young Kenyan runners now view marathon running as a feasible route to success, both monetary and social, thanks to his example. Many people have been inspired by Kipchoge's tale to begin running earlier in life with the hopes of one day surpassing his achievements. His accomplishments have also raised awareness of the expanding talent pool in Kenya's rural districts, which are home to many of the nation's best athletes. Kipchoge's story, in particular, has encouraged young runners from smaller areas to think that they can succeed internationally, which has helped to develop a new generation of talent across the nation.

The Creation of Infrastructure and Training Systems

The infrastructure that underpins Kenyan athletics has been impacted by Kipchoge. There is now more interest in developing better facilities and processes to develop youthful talent as a result of his training, discipline, and focus methods. Kipchoge's focus on a methodical, scientific approach to marathon training has benefited the introduction of structured coaching and access to top-notch training camps, especially in places like Eldoret and Iten.

The significance of environmental conditions in training has been further demonstrated by Kipchoge's time spent in high-altitude training facilities. Kipchoge trains in high-altitude areas of Kenya, which are now known across the world as ideal places for long-distance runners. Because of his influence, more funds are being allocated to developing the best training environments possible to help future Kenyan runners improve their skills.

An Example of Work Ethics and Discipline

The mindset of Kenyan athletes has also changed as a result of Kipchoge's impact. He is a prime example of the belief that perseverance, discipline, and humility are just as important to success as skill. For athletes of all skill levels, his regimen of rigorous self-discipline—early mornings, long training sessions, targeted diet, and rest—has become an inspiration. Kipchoge's perseverance and capacity to stay focused in the face of popularity and competition serve as a reminder that success comes from hard effort rather than shortcuts or diversions.

His unmatched level of professionalism in preparation and competition has also raised the bar for Kenyan athletes' approach to their sport. Kipchoge instills in the athletes he coaches the value of remaining grounded and focused instead of getting sidetracked by other influences. Knowing that Kipchoge's success was due to a deeply rooted work ethic rather than just physical skill, many aspiring Kenyan marathon runners now base their daily routines on his commitment to perfection.

Effects on the Nation's Economy

Due in part to Kipchoge's achievements, Kenya has become a global leader in distance running, which has increased economic opportunities for both individual athletes and the nation overall. Sponsorships, prize money, and a greater reputation in international contests have benefited marathoners, especially those who emulate Kipchoge. People from all over the world are visiting Kenya to take advantage of its high-altitude training facilities and running culture, which has helped the country's tourism industry.

Because of his financial success, Kipchoge has been able to assist numerous humanitarian causes and local educational initiatives in his community. Being one of the most well-known athletes in Kenya, his accomplishments have had a significant impact on the country's economy overall, especially for those working in the sports and athletic sectors.

Kenyan Athletics Promotion Worldwide

Kipchoge's global recognition has also raised awareness of Kenya's sports programs and the other gifted athletes coming out of the nation. Due to his widespread success, international race organizers now greatly value Kenyan marathoners, increasing the nation's prominence in international sports. Kenya has so established itself as a hub for athletic excellence by continuing to rule international championships in a range of long-distance events, not just marathon running.

Kenyan athletics has gained international recognition thanks to Kipchoge. Once mostly unknown outside of elite racing circles, the nation's runners are now well-known throughout the world for their work ethic, speed, and endurance. Global views of Kenyan athletics are still shaped by Kipchoge's influence, which has also encouraged runners everywhere to emulate him.

Legacy and Prolonged Impact

The impact of Eliud Kipchoge on Kenyan sports is extensive. Future generations of Kenyan runners will be shaped by his influence in terms of their goals, mindsets, and approaches to the sport. He has established a benchmark for quality, tenacity, and humility that will serve as a guide for upcoming marathon runners not only in Kenya but also worldwide.

Additionally, Kipchoge's impact is not limited to the sports world. He has demonstrated how important athletes can be in bringing about social change by using his position to promote topics like social development, sustainability, and education. His legacy is one of good influence, as his accomplishments have motivated not only athletes but also the Kenyan populace at large to set lofty objectives and pursue them with unwavering determination.

In the end, Eliud Kipchoge has made incalculable contributions to Kenyan sports. He has improved the sport, motivated the younger generation, and strengthened Kenya's reputation as the birthplace of the best distance runners in the world.

The Spirit of "No Human Is Limited"

"No Human Is Limited," Eliud Kipchoge's mantra, has evolved beyond a simple catchphrase to represent his philosophy, way of thinking, and approach to life and sports. Millions of people worldwide have been inspired by this straightforward yet impactful statement, which goes beyond sports to touch on deeper facets of human potential, tenacity, and the conviction that any goal—no matter how ambitious—is achievable.

The Origin of Philosophy

Kipchoge originally used the term "No Human Is Limited" as he was trying to break the two-hour marathon record, which many people thought was unachievable. Running a marathon in less than two hours was thought to be an impossible feat at the time, something that humans were incapable of completing. Kipchoge, however, resisted that restriction because of his unshakeable faith in the capacity of the human body and mind. His stance was unambiguous: the limitations that other people impose on us do not define our potential. It has no boundaries and is only constrained by our willpower, attitude, and capacity to overcome hardship.

Shattering Boundaries, Motivating the World

Not only did Kipchoge surpass the limits of physical endurance when he finished the INEOS 1:59 Challenge in 2019, but he also gained notoriety for his "No Human Is

Limited" philosophy. Even though the event was managed with pace teams and perfect circumstances, it was nevertheless a huge success that made it abundantly evident that the human spirit is more powerful than we realize. Kipchoge showed that we can overcome seemingly insurmountable obstacles if we have enough faith, commitment, and hard effort.

This accomplishment and the message it conveyed had an influence that went well beyond sports. Kipchoge's words inspired people from various walks of life, including athletes, business owners, students, and those going through difficult times. "No Human Is Limited" became a catchphrase for those who were chasing their own goals, inspiring them to overcome both internal and external constraints.

Living Out the Spirit in Daily Life

This attitude is more than just running, according to Kipchoge. It involves accepting the difficulties life presents, meeting them head-on, and realizing that mental toughness is the key to success. The main takeaway is always the same, whether it's an athlete trying to set new marks or a person dealing with personal struggles: the biggest obstacles we encounter are frequently self-imposed. Kipchoge has exemplified this idea by continuously surpassing expectations, setting records, and demonstrating that perseverance and belief are more powerful than natural skill alone in achieving success.

A Challenge to Typical Boundaries

Kipchoge has consistently questioned the notion of human limitations. In a society where many people think that some things are impossible, Kipchoge's performances have caused people to reevaluate what is feasible. He has reinterpreted the marathon as a test of human will as much as a competition. We are frequently more capable than we realize, as evidenced by his capacity to force our body to function at its peak for extended periods.

Kipchoge has continuously demonstrated in training and competition that the body's capacity is unbounded by external barriers. His conviction that the human body has boundless potential has inspired many athletes and people to ask themselves: What else could I accomplish if I refused to accept limitations? Pushing the limits of human ability in sports and other fields has become a global discussion sparked by Kipchoge's philosophy.

A Source of Motivation for Upcoming Generations

"No Human Is Limited" leaves a legacy that goes well beyond Kipchoge's achievements. It has evolved into a guiding concept for a new generation of athletes and aspirants who recognize that real greatness comes from conquering social, mental, and physical challenges. Kipchoge's narrative provides a model for achievement by demonstrating that obstacles are chances to push oneself to the limit.

His accomplishments have demonstrated that greatness is more about how one handles difficulties than it is about beginning with the best conditions or assets. It all comes down to belief—belief in the process, in oneself, and in the potential to exceed every barrier. Kipchoge's message strikes a deep chord, particularly in a world where uncertainty and doubt frequently erect imperceptible barriers that impede progress.

The Legacy of Infinity

Eliud Kipchoge's "No Human Is Limited" concept is a way of life rather than only a phrase. His deeds and words encourage others to see past their apparent boundaries and acknowledge that we are all capable of success. Kipchoge's journey has shown that human potential is not limited by what other people think is achievable. His life story—from being raised in a small rural village to becoming a world-class marathon runner—is a living example of the notion that the only boundaries we set for ourselves are those we set for ourselves.

Kipchoge's legacy will live on as long as he inspires people all over the world with his performances and his unflinching faith in the strength of the human spirit. The timeless message of "No Human Is Limited" will continue to inspire athletes and aspirants alike to rise to the occasion, push themselves, and never give up on their dreams of success.

Conclusion

Eliud Kipchoge's transformation from a small Kenyan town to the world's finest marathon runner is a stirring example of self-control, tenacity, and an unwavering faith in human potential. In addition to pushing the boundaries of long-distance running with his record-breaking performances, Olympic victories, and the historic sub-two-hour marathon, Kipchoge has motivated others all around the world to pursue their own goals, no matter how lofty they may seem.

His slogan, "No Human Is Limited," is embodied throughout his life. Kipchoge's legacy endures in the hearts of people he has inspired to overcome fear, push boundaries, and trust in the strength of perseverance—it goes far beyond the finish lines he has passed. Eliud Kipchoge has demonstrated that anything is achievable with the correct mindset in his roles as an athlete, mentor, and worldwide role model. His tale will inspire future generations and serve as a constant reminder that when we don't let limitations stop us, greatness is possible.

Printed in Dunstable, United Kingdom

72967331R00050